Viola Time Runners

Viola accompaniment book

Kathy and David Blackwell

OXFORD
UNIVERSITY PRESS

OXFORD

UNIVERSITY PRESS

Great Clarendon Street, Oxford OX2 6DP,
United Kingdom

Oxford University Press is a department of the University of Oxford.
It furthers the University's objective of excellence in research, scholarship,
and education by publishing worldwide. Oxford is a registered trade mark of
Oxford University Press in the UK and in certain other countries

ISBN 978-019-356621-7

Cover illustration by Martin Remphry

Music and text origination Katie Johnston and Julia Bovee
Printed in Great Britain

Contents

1.	Start the show	4
2.	Banyan tree	5
3.	Heat haze	6
4.	Medieval tale	7
5.	In memory	8
6.	Chase in the dark	9
7.	Merrily danced the Quaker's wife	10
8.	O leave your sheep	11
9.	Jingle bells (J. Pierpont)	12
10.	Allegretto in C (Mozart)	13
11.	The Mallow fling	14
12.	Noël (Daquin)	15
13.	Finale from the 'Water Music' (Handel)	16
14.	Ecossaise in G (Beethoven)	17
15.	Viola Time rag	18
16.	Busy day (*duet*)	20
17.	On the go!	21
18.	Blue whale	22
19.	Takin' it easy	24
20.	Mean street chase	23
21.	Ten thousand miles away	28
22.	I got those viola blues	26
23.	Air in C (J. C. Bach)	27
24.	Prelude from 'Te Deum' (Charpentier)	29
25.	That's how it goes!	30
26.	Flamenco dance	32
27.	Somebody's knocking at your door	31
28.	The old chariot	33
29.	Adam in the garden	34
30.	Air (Handel)	36
31.	The wee cooper o' Fife	37
32.	Aerobics!	38
33.	Caribbean sunshine	39

1. Start the show

KB & DB

2. Banyan tree

C string special

Jamaican folk tune

3. Heat haze

KB & DB

Relaxed

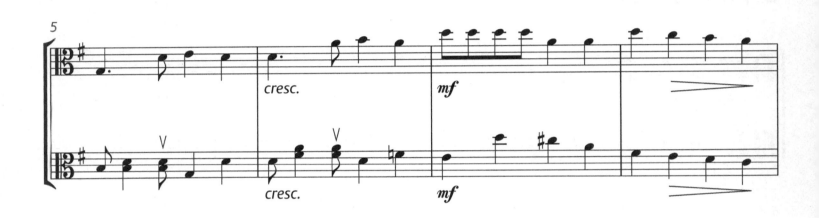

4. Medieval tale

KB & DB

5. In memory

KB & DB

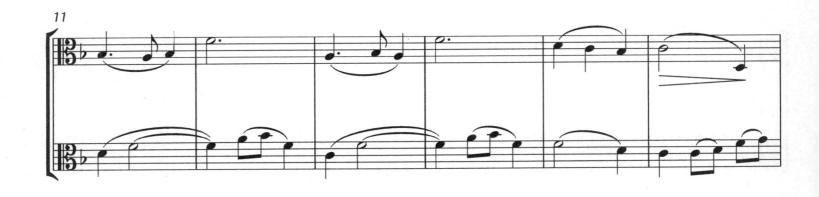

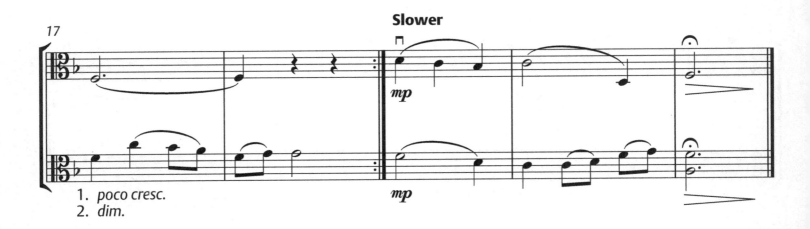

1. poco cresc.
2. dim.

6. Chase in the dark

KB & DB

With menace

7. Merrily danced the Quaker's wife

Scottish folk tune

8. O leave your sheep

C string special

French folk tune

9. Jingle bells

J. Pierpont

The introduction is not included in the pupil's book; thus, bar numbers given here follow the numbering in the pupil's book and the D.C. al Fine is written as a D.% al Fine.

10. Allegretto in C

11. The Mallow fling

Irish folk tune

12. Noël

Daquin

Allegretto

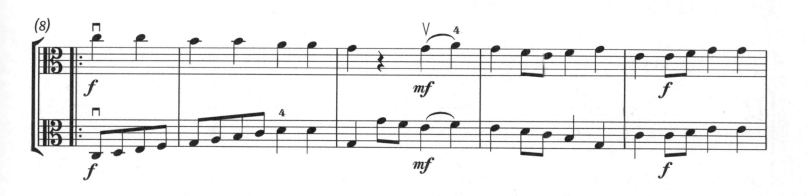

13. Finale from the 'Water Music'

Handel

14. Ecossaise in G

Beethoven

15. Viola Time rag

KB & DB

Not too fast

18

16. Busy day

KB & DB

17. On the go!

KB & DB

18. Blue whale

C string special

KB & DB

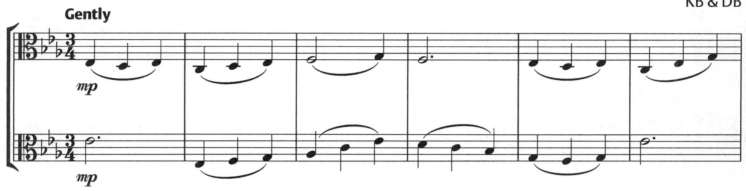

22

19. Takin' it easy: next page

20. Mean street chase

C string special

KB & DB

Funky

Nos. 19 and 20 are reversed to avoid a page turn.

19. Takin' it easy

KB & DB

Laid-back tempo

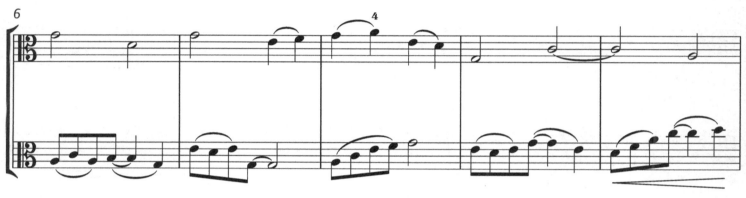

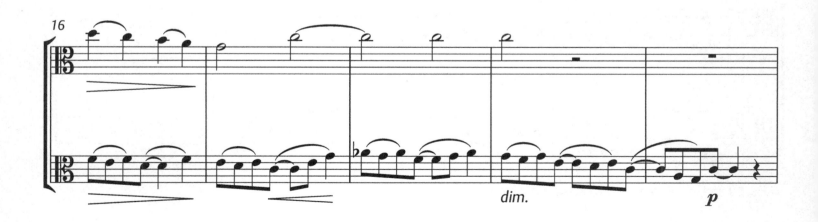

21. Ten thousand miles away: page 28

22. I got those viola blues

KB & DB

No. 21 is shown on page 28 to avoid a page turn in No. 22.

23. Air in C

J. C. Bach

21. Ten thousand miles away

With a good swing

Sea shanty

24. Prelude from 'Te Deum'

Charpentier

25. That's how it goes!

KB & DB

30

26. *Flamenco dance:* next page

27. Somebody's knocking at your door

Spiritual

Nos. 26 and 27 are reversed to avoid a page turn.

26. Flamenco dance

KB & DB

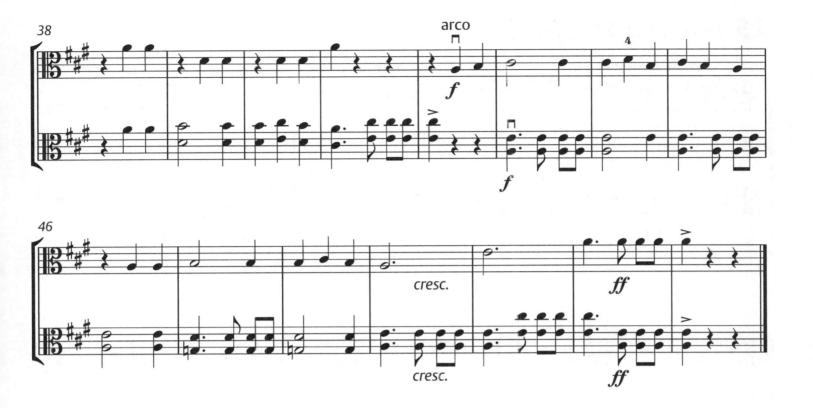

28. The old chariot

Sea shanty

29. Adam in the garden

Jamaican folk tune

30. Air

Handel

31. The wee cooper o' Fife

Scottish folk tune

32. Aerobics!

KB & DB

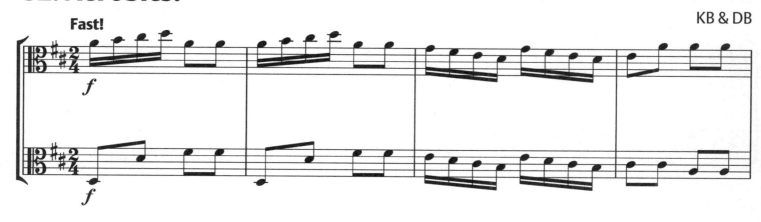

33. Caribbean sunshine

KB & DB